Dragons

Other titles in the Monsters and Mythical Creatures series include:

Aliens
Cyclops
Demons
Goblins
Water Monsters
Zombies

Dragons

Carla Mooney

San Diego, CA

Printed in the United States

For more information, contact:
ReferencePoint Press, Inc.
PO Box 27779
San Diego, CA 92198
www. ReferencePointPress.com

LIBRARY OF CONGRESS CATALOGING-IN-PUBLICATION DATA

Mooney, Carla, 1970–
Dragons / by Carla Mooney.
p. cm. — (Monsters and mythical creatures)
Includes bibliographical references and index.
ISBN-13: 978-1-60152-148-4 (hardback)
ISBN-10: 1-60152-148-0 (hardback)
1. Dragons. I. Title.
GR830.D7M66 2011
398.24'54—dc22

2010027313

Contents

Introduction

The Mystery of Dragons

In the early 1600s, British cleric and author Edward Topsell painstakingly catalogued hundreds of animals. With detailed descriptions and drawings or woodcuts, he carefully recorded in two volumes what each animal looked like, how it behaved, and where it lived. Topsell's *Historie of Foure-footed Beastes, Describing the True and Lively Figure of Every Beast*, published in 1607, and *Historie of Serpents; or, the Second Booke of Living Creatures*, published in 1608, are based in large part on earlier published animal collections and, he notes, on "the testimonies of sundry learned men."[1]

Tucked between descriptions of everyday animals such as cats, horses, and snakes, Topsell includes fantastic illustrations and descriptions of the winged dragon and other mythical creatures. Topsell writes that dragons are reptiles and closely related to serpents. He illustrates the winged dragon complete with two large wings; scaly skin; sharp claws; a long, whiplike tail; and sharp teeth. He also describes dragon behavior: "Dragons abide in deep Caves and hollow places of the earth, and . . . sometimes when they perceive [motions] in the air, they come out of their holes and beating the air with their wings, as it were with the strokes of Oars, they forsake the earth and flie aloft."[2]

Did You Know?

Dragon tales and legends can be found on every continent except Antarctica.

In addition, Topsell notes that dragons enjoy eating lettuce but avoid apples because they cause upset stomachs.

Today, people know that dragons are an invention of human imagination. Centuries ago, however, dragons were thought to be as real as pigs or chickens or rats. Authorities repeated and circulated stories of dragon encounters, and thus those stories were perceived as true. Even into the seventeenth century, scholars and scientists wrote about dragons as if they were living creatures. European biologists and Chinese scholars alike described in detail the appearance, behavior, and habitat of dragons. Even though many, including Topsell, had never seen a dragon with their own eyes, it did not make dragons any less real to them. "And this which I have written, may be sufficient to satisfie any reasonable man, that there are winged Serpents and Dragons in the world,"[3] writes Topsell.

In two volumes published in the early 1600s cleric Edward Topsell painstakingly catalogued hundreds of animals, providing detailed descriptions and illustrations of each. A page from Topsell's collection, featuring three types of dragons, appears here.

Real or Imaginary?

This view of dragons is not limited to one country or period of time. Dragon stories exist in almost every culture and continent. In

the West, ancient Greek mythology tells of immense, malevolent dragons that battle heroes and gods. In Asia, Chinese manuscripts dating to around 2700 B.C. describe dragons that grow beards and carry magical pearls. Serpentlike dragons slither through the folklore of India and the Americas. European travelers who visited Africa and Asia in the 1600s brought back remarkably detailed reports of dragon sightings. Though few people actually claimed to have seen a live dragon themselves, many unquestioningly passed along tales of other people's encounters.

Did You Know?

A 1658 single-volume reprint of Edward Topsell's two books contains 175 entries, beginning with "Antalope" and ending with "Viper."

By the nineteenth century, however, doubts arose about the existence of dragons. Victorian naturalists traveled the globe, searching for evidence of dragons. Although they encountered some giant snakes and lizards, they did not discover a single fire-breathing, winged dragon.

From that point, the dragon took its place in the realm of imaginary beasts. "How much better it would have been if only some of them had turned out to be real living and breathing creatures that we could, at great risk and with enormous difficulty, encounter and marvel at today,"[4] says British zoologist Desmond Morris.

Origins of the Dragon Myth

Researchers often ponder the origins of imaginary beasts that somehow find their way into the lore of cultures and countries around the world. Dragons are one of many such creatures whose existence has never been proved and yet seem to be part of a body of shared human knowledge. Although dragon stories place the beasts in ancient times, prehistoric cave art shows no signs of such creatures. In addition, descriptions of the dragon from different ages and cultures are eerily similar. How could so many cultures, noted for their differences, create the same fantastic creature? Historians and experts in dragon myths have sought to understand and explain the reasons behind these similarities.

Experts have two theories about the origins of the dragon myth. Some believe dragons were first envisioned from serpents, water creatures, and other reptiles in the ancient Near East. From there, dragon stories grew and spread to India and China. Spreading farther, these stories evolved into the dragons of Greek mythology, Christian lore, and Western literature.

A second theory suggests that dragon myths emerged independently in many different places, reflecting a universal human fear of snakes, reptiles, and serpents. As ancient cultures spread and came into contact with each other, these myths began to merge and influence each other.

A Fearsome and Wondrous Beast

Whether real or imaginary, the dragon is one of the most fascinating creatures in recorded history. According to *Dragons* author Peter Hogarth, dragons "have instilled fear and wonder in the minds and hearts of men since the dawn of history."[5] In some stories, dragons are portrayed as wise guardians; in others, they are nightmarish monsters. Much of what people today think about dragons comes from these centuries-old stories and accounts. From ancient myths and legends to modern movies and books, the dragon has become one of the most well-known legendary beasts of all time.

Chapter 1

The Legendary Beast

Though stories of dragons come from all parts of the globe and from many different periods of time, the descriptions are surprisingly similar. In most portrayals, the dragon is a giant reptilelike creature with a long tail. A thick neck stretches from its muscular body. Heavy scales line and protect the dragon's body from head to tail. The dragon's legs end in sharp talons that can rip the flesh from its prey. Some dragons have spikes running down their spines and horns protruding from their heads. Many dragons have huge wings for flying.

A Body Built for Battle

The most important part of the dragon's defense is its thick layer of scales. The scales form armor that protects the dragon's body against attack. In the epic poem *Beowulf*, when King Beowulf slices at the dragon with his sword, it glances off the dragon's scales, leaving the dragon unharmed. Dragon mythology also explains that unlike a snake, a dragon does not shed its entire skin at one time. Instead, a dragon grows new scales underneath the old, shedding small sections of scales at a time. This keeps the majority of its body armor intact at any given time.

Not only is a dragon's body built for protection, it is also equipped to attack. In many myths, a dragon uses its sharp claws to slash its prey. Its large, sharp teeth easily rip into its next meal or enemy. One swipe from a dragon's heavy, powerful tail can knock an enemy down.

Vulnerable Underbelly

A small, unprotected section, however, can leave a dragon vulnerable. In one legend from Scandinavia, a monstrous dragon named Fafnir succumbs to a sword strike to the underbelly. In the story, Fafnir jealously hides gold in a cave and guards the treasure night and day.

The dragons of legend are often huge reptilian beasts with thick necks and muscular bodies; long, spiked tails; and sharp talons. Though formidable foes in battle, according to many stories, they have a vulnerable underbelly.

Fafnir was born a dwarf, but greed slowly transformed him into a dragon. Fafnir's dwarf brother, Regin, secretly wants Fafnir's gold. Promising to share the treasure, Regin convinces a young knight named Sigurd to attack the dragon.

Fafnir's magnificent scales protect him from most weapons, but his naked belly is vulnerable. Using a sword made by Regin, Sigurd digs a deep pit along the path to a stream where Fafnir travels for his daily drink of water. There Sigurd lies in the pit, until he hears Fafnir slithering overhead. Dragon expert and author Peter Hogarth describes what happens next.

> And when the dragon crawled to the water, the earth shuddered and the land all around shook. He breathed out poison all over the path ahead. However, Sigurd was neither frightened nor dismayed. When the dragon crawled across his pit, Sigurd thrust in his sword under the left shoulder, and it sank in up to the hilt. Then he leaped out of the pit, wrenching back his sword, and getting his arms bloody right up to the shoulders. And when the huge dragon felt its death wound, it lashed with its tail and head, shattering everything that got in its way. And then Fafnir died."[6]

Did You Know?

Like the dragon in the Old English epic poem *Beowulf*, some dragons protect their treasure with a curse, bringing ill to those who would steal from them.

In one retelling of the Danish legend of King Frotho and the Island Dragons, a young King Frotho kills a fierce dragon by attacking its soft underbelly. Frotho is searching for riches to pay for his country's military operations. One day while on this quest, Frotho overhears a local farmer singing about a nearby island where a dragon hides deep within a mountain, guarding a vast treasure. Intrigued, Frotho asks the farmer where he could find this dragon and its treasure. The farmer warns young Frotho of the monster whose "three-pronged tongue flickers from its mouth, and its mouth spews horrific danger; but do not be dissuaded by its razor-sharp teeth, nor by the strength of its coils, nor by the venom it spews from its mouth."[7]

Color of a Dragon

Dragons come in a rainbow of colors. In some legends, the color of a dragon is an outward sign of its temperament. Primary color dragons such as black or red are more likely to be evil. Black dragons are said to be vile, evil tempered, and surrounded by death. Red dragons often represent greed and are obsessed with increasing their treasure. Blue dragons are said to represent vanity and often live in hot, desertlike climates. Green dragons, which prefer to live in forests, are rude and sneaky.

Unlike primary color dragons, metallic-looking dragons are more good-natured, especially in modern fantasy literature. They generally will not fight unless provoked. The five kinds of metallic dragons are: brass, bronze, copper, gold, and silver. Among these friendlier beasts, the bronze dragon usually lives near deep water and has a strong sense of justice. Gold dragons often embark on quests to promote good. The most sensitive of the metallic dragons, the silver dragon, enjoys helping the weak and healing the injured.

Despite the farmer's warning, Frotho travels to the dragon's cave and stabs the beast with his sword. The dragon's thick hide protects it from Frotho's attack—until Frotho remembers the soft spot on the dragon's underbelly and thus kills it. Afterward, Frotho collects the dragon's treasure and sails away a wealthy man.

Deadly Breath

Perhaps the most dangerous and recognizable weapon in the dragon's arsenal is its ability to breathe fire. In many myths, it can shoot a blast of fire to scorch objects and prey hundreds of yards away. Some dragons blow poisonous fumes, smoke, venom, or acid that can kill a person or animal. Edward Topsell notes in his 1607 book that dragons "with the force of their breath do draw the Birds that flie over their heads into their throat . . . some vaporous and venomous breath is sent up from the Dragon to them, that [poisoneth] and infecteth the air about them, whereby their senses are taken from them, and they astonished fall down into his mouth."[8]

Myths and legends do not explain how a dragon is able to breathe fire. The creators of the Animal Planet special, *Dragons: A Fantasy Made Real*, collaborated with dragon expert and biologist Peter Hogarth to develop one possible theory. They suggest that a dragon could breathe fire if it produces large amounts of hydrogen gas, which it stores in sacs in its body. To create a fiery blast, the dragon would blow out the easily burned hydrogen. To light the hydrogen, the dragon would grind a mineral such as platinum between its teeth. The platinum would produce a spark that lights the hydrogen gas.

Stories of fire-breathing dragons instilled fear in people of ancient times for they had no means of protection against such a dangerous weapon. Only the bravest souls, usually knights or other warriors, dared to confront dragons.

Soaring into the Sky

A fearsome hunter on the ground, the legendary dragon can also track its prey from the air. There it hunts like a bird of prey, swoop-

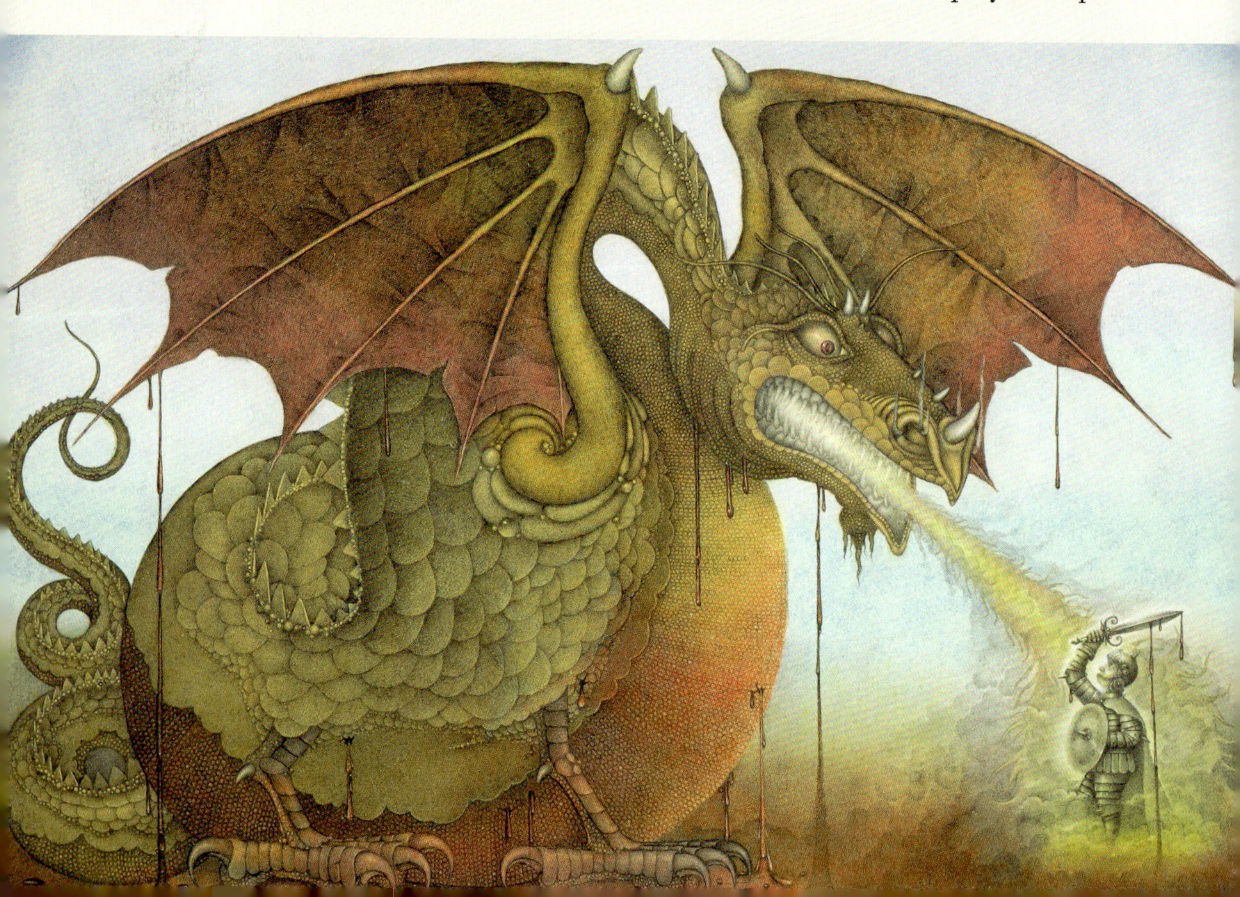

ing in to grab deer, sheep, goats, or people. In Chinese and Japanese myths, a dragon flies magically in the air, even though it does not have wings.

The idea of a dragon gracefully lifting into the air in flight might seem at odds with its thick, heavy, muscular body. Some dragon experts pondered this idea; they have a theory of how this might be possible. The dragon's bones would have to be similar to the bones of a bird. Instead of heavy, dense bones like humans, the dragon would have hollow bones with a honeycomb pattern inside. This would make the bones strong, but lightweight. It also would create a frame strong enough to lift the dragon's body into flight.

Did You Know?

In Ancient China, fat from a dragon was thought to be useful for waterproofing silk garments.

In many myths and legends, one of the most recognizable features of a flying dragon is its immense and powerful wings. Some stories describe dragons with batlike wings that have a leathery skin stretched over fingerlike bones. Other stories report dragons with birdlike wings covered in feathers.

Infinite Variety

When imagining a dragon, most people picture a traditional beast with four legs, clawed feet, and beating wings. Yet several different types of dragons are described in folklore and legends. In legends from Africa, the wyvern is the largest of all dragons and is commonly said to roam the continent's deserts and savannahs. The wyvern has two large wings and two feet that end in eaglelike talons. The European dragon is similar to the wyvern and often makes its home in the mountains. Stories from Europe speak of a dragon with four legs, large batlike wings, and a long tail whose tip is shaped like an arrowhead. In other tales, the frost dragon lives in bitterly cold and icy places. This dragon is similar in size and appearance to the European dragon, but it can instantly freeze enemies with its icy breath.

The folklore of China and Japan depict wingless dragons, which are now described as Asian dragons. Often, the Asian dragon carries a large, magic pearl that gives it the ability to fly.

Stories from the plains and steppes of the Americas, North Africa, and Europe sometimes describe the *amphiptere* as a legless, winged dragon. One of the earliest records of the *amphiptere* comes from ancient Egypt, where it guards frankincense trees in great swarms. The Egyptians describe this beast as having eyes like the feathers in a peacock's tail and wings that sparkle and glitter when it flies.

Did You Know?

In China, travelers who had eaten roasted swallow were advised not to cross water right after eating because roasted swallow was thought to be a favorite meal of dragons.

In North America, the Algonquin Indians worshipped a dragonlike creature they called the *piasa,* or "the bird that devours human beings." In 1673 explorer Father Jacques Marquette spotted petroglyphs, carved and painted into a cliff face above the Mississippi River. According to Father Marquette's Indian guide, these petroglyphs showed a terrible dragon that had once lived in the region. According to Father Marquette's diary, the *piasa* "was as large as a calf with horns like a deer, red eyes, a beard like a tiger's, a face like a man, the body covered with green, red and black scales and a tail so long it passed around the body, over the head and between the legs."[9]

Grounded Dragons

Some stories describe dragons that cannot fly. These dragons are more like serpents than traditional winged dragons. Some like the *knucker* from England have tiny wings that are not used in flight. Others like the *lindorm* do not have wings at all. The *lindorm* is commonly featured in stories from the mountainous regions of eastern and northern Europe. In a retelling of the Swedish legend *The Bride of the Lindorm King*, "the queen had given birth to a lindorm, a hideous, snakelike dragon, whose wingless body thrashed upon the marble floor in scaly coils, and from whose shoulders sprang a pair of powerful limbs with taloned feet."[10]

Stories of water dragons that cannot fly are also common in India, Scandinavia, and North America. These dragons are expert swimmers that scour the seas and lakes for underwater prey. They may be related to the mysterious beasts in sea serpent myths. In fact, some people believe that Scotland's legendary Loch Ness Monster, a long-necked lake monster, is really a water dragon.

The Dragon's Lair

Dragons can live almost anywhere, from the highest mountaintops to the deepest seas. In most stories, however, dragons are depicted as solitary creatures, coming together with other dragons only to mate or fight for territory. Most prefer an enclosed lair that gives them a safe place to sleep for days or months at a time. Some dragons live in deep, underground caverns. Others live in swamps, abandoned castles, or remote mountainside caves. In Asian myths, dragons swim to underwater caves at the bottom of oceans, lakes,

While many dragons of legend have powerful wings, others look more like serpents. Though unable to fly, these snakelike dragons have powerful limbs and taloned feet with which to protect themselves or do battle.

Monster Cousins: The Neo Dragons

Several mythical creatures are closely related to and sometimes mistaken for dragons. The mistaken identity is not surprising as these beasts share several similar behaviors and characteristics with their dragon cousins.

Basilisk: This small reptile was once one of the most feared monsters in the Western world. Scholar Pliny the Elder from the first century A.D. described the basilisk as a snake with a golden crown. In fact, the name *basilisk* is Greek for "little king." It can kill the largest animal with a single glance. Its poison breath wilts vegetation and shatters boulders. It was also believed that if a man on horseback tried to kill a basilisk with a spear, the monster's poison would travel up the spear, killing both man and horse.

Cockatrice: According to myth, the cockatrice is born from a hen's egg hatched by a serpent or toad. It develops into a monster with the body of a serpent and the head and legs of a rooster. It evolved from early descriptions of the basilisk and shares its ability to kill with a glance or with poisonous breath.

Hydra: Known from Greek mythology, the hydra has a serpent's body with many dragonlike heads, usually nine. If one head is severed, two grow back in its place. It can kill with its poisonous venom and bone-crunching jaws. The Greek hero Hercules defeated a hydra during his adventures.

and rivers. Frost dragons inhabit ice caves hollowed out from the side of a glacier or iceberg.

In many stories, dragons collect and guard treasure deep inside lairs. Most of the time, legends say, dragons fly around the world, picking up items from different places and bringing them home to their lairs. The treasure can be gold coins, silver cups, or a rainbow of colored gems. The jewels and coins sometimes stick to the dragon's soft underbelly and become a glittering armor against attack. Asian dragons collect jade, opals, and pearls. Some dragons, like the *knucker*, collect shiny items, like pieces of glass or marbles. Other dragons highly value magical objects such as enchanted swords or magical rings. Some dragons choose to guard a single enchanted item instead of an entire cave of treasure.

One of the easiest ways to provoke a mythical dragon is to steal a piece of its treasure. In the Greek tale Jason and the Golden Fleece, the hero Jason returns to the city of Iolus to claim his late father's throne. His uncle promises him the throne if he delivers a rare treasure, the golden fleece found on the island of Colchis. The fleece is very valuable as it has magical healing powers. No one had been able to reach the fleece because a fierce dragon guards the magical treasure. After traveling to the farthest eastern corner of the Black Sea, Jason arrives at Colchis. With help from King Aeetes' daughter Medea, he discovers the grove where the fleece lies hidden. When Jason approaches the golden fleece, a tremendous battle takes place between the young man and the dragon. Aided by a magic potion from Medea, Jason lulls the dragon to sleep and kills it. Then he claims his prize, the golden fleece.

Did You Know?

A dragon's fire was said to reach a staggering 1,000 degrees Fahrenheit (378 degrees Celsius). Thick layers of mucus would have protected the dragon's mouth from being burned by its own fiery breath.

Dragon Magic

In addition to physical strength, a dragon often has magical powers. In some stories, dragons can read minds. Other stories show dragons that can shape-shift, or change their appearance. Still others tell of dragons that can paralyze victims simply by staring them in the eye. Some dragons have special healing powers that they use to help sick or injured humans.

In some stories, dragons receive their powers from a magical object such as a jewel that they wear or have embedded in their bodies.

In this illustration of the famous story from Greek mythology, Jason and the Golden Fleece, Jason confronts the dragon that guards the magical golden fleece. With the help of a magic potion, Jason puts the beast to sleep, then kills it and claims the fleece.

Chinese dragons often carry a magical pearl that is believed to give them power and allow them to ascend into heaven. The pearl also bestows its magical powers on humans who possess one. In one Chinese legend, a young man named Tchang lives with his mother on the banks of a great lake where no fish swim. On a journey, he encounters a dragon with a gleaming pearl in its forehead. In exchange for a favor, the dragon gives Tchang the pearl. With the pearl, Tchang is able to grow fruit on barren trees, cause a mute girl to speak, and give sight to his blind mother. The magic pearl also brings fish to the lake by Tchang's home and makes the surrounding land fertile.

Magical Healing Powers

In the past, people who believed in dragons and their magic also thought that dragon parts such as bones, teeth, and blood had magical or healing properties. This belief was so widespread that ancient texts gave recipes for preparing dragon parts. Historian Lei Hiao, who lived in China from A.D. 420–477, left the following instructions:

> To use dragon's bone first cook aromatic herbs. Wash the bone twice in hot water, then reduce it to powder and place it in bags of thin stuff [cloth]. Take two young swallows, and after removing their entrails, stuff the bags into the swallows and hang them over a spring. After one night, take the bags out of the swallows, remove the powder, and mix it with a preparation for strengthening the kidneys. The effect of such a medicine is as if it were divine.[11]

In China, powdered dragon bone was considered to be an effective cure for many illnesses, including dysentery, gallstones, fever, and paralysis of the legs. In the West, people believed that spreading dragon blood over skin could make a person invulnerable to all

wounds. They also thought that a dragon's eyes could be used to make an ointment that gave courage to those who applied it.

Legends spread the belief that eating a dragon's heart will allow a person to understand animals. In the legend of Sigurd and Fafnir, the dwarf Regin asks Sigurd to cut out the dragon's heart and roast it. As Sigurd passes the roasted heart to the dwarf, he burns his fingers. Licking them, he tastes part of the dragon's heart. Instantly, Sigurd understands the chatter of birds overhead who tell him that Regin plans to double-cross him. The dwarf is plotting to kill Sigurd for his share of the dragon's treasure. Sigurd heeds the birds' warning, beheads Regin, and claims the treasure as his own.

Many people also believed that a dragon's teeth held special powers. Worn on clothing, dragon teeth would provide protection against all evils. The Chinese believed that grinding dragon teeth into a fine powder and ingesting it would bring health and vitality. Ancient Greek myths claim that dragon teeth could be planted in the ground to grow an army of warriors. In one tale, the hero Cadmus fights and kills a dragon. The goddess Athena tells Cadmus to take the dragon's teeth and sow half of them into the soil as if they were seeds of corn. Cadmus plants the teeth and immediately they sprout into fierce, armed men. These warriors become known as the Spartoi or "sown men." Cadmus throws a stone at the men, who turn on each other and begin to fight. When only five remain alive, Cadmus places them under his command and founds the Greek city of Thebes. These five remaining Spartoi become the founders of the noble families of Thebes.

Did You Know?

Dragons were once believed to have the best sight of any animal.

Man's Enemy

With its fearsome body and mysterious magical powers, the dragon became man's powerful enemy in a variety of myths and legends. The tenth-century poem *Beowulf* describes one of the most famous struggles between man and dragon. In the epic poem, a dragon emerges to threaten the aging King Beowulf's realm. Each night, the dragon terrorizes and destroys the countryside, breathing fire over houses, farms, and fields. King Beowulf wonders why the dragon has come, bent on destroying his kingdom. After weeks of fire and destruction, one of the king's servants confesses that he stole a jeweled cup from the dragon's lair. That night, the dragon began its nightly raids.

To save his kingdom, the king gathers a troop of men and heads to face the dragon in battle. When they reach the dragon's lair, all of the men flee in fear except Beowulf's kinsman Wiglaf. Beowulf climbs into the cave's mouth and shouts a challenge to the monster. The sleeping dragon awakes and answers with a stream of flame as it flies into the air. The dragon circles, and then descends to attack Beowulf.

Beowulf's iron shield protects him from the dragon's fiery breath. The king strikes the dragon with his sword, but the iron blade glances off the dragon's scales. The dragon regroups for a second attack. This time Wiglaf steps forward to help his king, but his wooden shield is no match for the dragon's flames. Wiglaf huddles with Beowulf under the king's iron shield. Beowulf strikes at the dragon again, his sword shattering on the scales.

For a third time, the dragon attacks, biting Beowulf's neck with sharp fangs. Blood gushes from Beowulf's wound, covering him. Wiglaf rushes to save his lord, and drives a giant sword through the monster's unprotected belly into its heart. The dragon's fiery breath weakens, and Beowulf again attacks the dragon's belly with a battle knife. Finally, the dragon falls. The king and Wiglaf had slain the monster. Their victory, however, is not without a price. The king is mortally wounded. As dragon poison quickly works through his body, the old warrior dies.

Through ancient stories like *Beowulf*, the dragon has emerged as one of the most powerful and mysterious legendary creatures. Dragons have inspired and terrorized people throughout history—and will continue to do so for some time to come.

Chapter 2

Deadly Dragons of the West

The myths and folklore of Europe and the Middle East usually depict dragons as deadly and terrifying. These Western dragons, as they are known, are typically large, scaly creatures that resemble dinosaurs or large lizards. They usually breathe fire, have wings designed for flight, and live in cave, mountain, or forest hideaways. Often dragons are portrayed as clever and cunning, having intelligence equal to humans.

In many tales, Western dragons represent the darker side of humans. They are often shown as greedy, vain, malicious, and violent. Therefore, many Western myths tell of the struggle between people and dragons, in a classic good vs. evil fight. Often a brave warrior or glorious god battles and defeats a deadly dragon. Western myths also use dragons to explain nature and the origins of mountains, rivers, and other places. In still other tales, dragons have a central role in the creation of the earth and all the life upon it.

Tiamat and Marduk

One of the earliest Western dragon myths, recorded on clay tablets nearly 4,000 years ago, comes from the ancient Babylonians. Their story is a creation myth that explains the origins of the earth and humans. According to that story, before the earth was created, a ferocious female dragon named Tiamat reigned in terror. She was the god of saltwater and chaos. Karl Shuker, a zoologist who researches and writes about mythological creatures, describes

Tiamat as a "serpentine horror with impervious scales, two powerful muscular forelegs whose feet were equipped with dagger-like talons, a long neck held proudly erect, and a pair of curved horns upon her head."[12]

Angry when new gods killed her mate Apsu, the male god of freshwater and space, Tiamat raged and destroyed all who challenged her. The valiant sun god Marduk agreed to do battle with Tiamat. He armed himself with an immense net to capture her and bow and arrows to slay her. During the battle, Marduk shot an arrow straight into Tiamat's mouth that landed inside her unprotected belly. After the monster died, Marduk stood proudly over her corpse as the supreme power in the universe.

With the passing of Tiamat, Marduk created the world. In his retelling of the myth, Shuker describes Marduk's actions. "After cleaving her body in two, he fashioned one half into the heavens, and molded the other into the earth. He set the stars in the heavens and garnished the earth with fields, forests, rivers, and mountains, populating them with a teeming myriad of wildlife." From Tiamat's dragon blood, Marduk created humanity, "a race born from blood and destined to spill so much of its own in the ages to come."[13]

Egyptian Serpent Dragons

In ancient Egypt the people told of Apophis, a powerful, destructive god that existed from the beginning of time. Apophis is a huge serpentlike monster that represents darkness and chaos. He is the enemy of creation and wants to devour the sun. Each night after the sun sets, the sun god Ra sails the great solar ship through the underworld. As dawn nears and Ra is returning with the sun from the underworld, Apophis attacks.

Most days, Ra and the other gods fight off the evil monster, and the sun once again rises in the sky. Other times, however, Apophis succeeds and swallows the ship whole. His victory never lasts, and the gods are eventually able to cut the solar ship from his belly and return it to the sky. Scholars believe

Did You Know?

On the grounds of the United Nations building in New York stands a statue titled *Good Defeats Evil.* It portrays the third-century Roman soldier Saint George slaying a dragon.

that the story of Apophis may have been used by ancient Egyptians to explain why the sun was blacked out during a solar eclipse.

Dragons in Greek Mythology

After the decline of ancient Egypt, Greek civilization arose and flourished between 2000 B.C. and 146 B.C. Many of the best-known Western dragon stories come from this time. In fact, the word *dragon* comes from the Greek word "drakon." Serpentlike monsters appear in the story of Medusa, the adventures of Hercules, and in the battles of the gods.

In one myth, the god Zeus has an epic battle with the great dragon Typhon. One account describes Typhon this way: "in size and strength he surpassed all offspring of . . . Earth, towering over the mountains and occasionally brushing the stars with his head. From head to thighs, he approximated human form, but sprouting a hundred dragons' heads and numerous wings; his lower limbs were huge coiling serpents. So awesome was he that when the gods first saw him they all fled."[14]

Zeus alone stands to face the dragon. Shooting fire, Typhon attacks Mount Olympus. The battle between the two rages and Zeus meets Typhon's attack with thunderbolts. Typhon wraps his coils around Zeus and cuts out the muscles from Zeus's arms and legs. He casts Zeus into the caves of Cilicia. With help from the god Hermes, Zeus reassembles his arms and legs and emerges from the caves stronger than ever. He throws lightning bolts at Typhon until he mortally wounds the monster. Then Zeus piles rock and earth upon Typhon, trapping him under the island of Sicily.

Did You Know?

Western dragons often symbolize the destructive effects of wealth and power.

Sicily, located at the southern tip of Italy, was known in ancient times for its many earthquakes and for the massive volcano, called Mount Etna, which erupted from time to time. The mythical battle between Zeus and the dragon Typhon, and Typhon's ultimate defeat, gave the people of the time a way of understanding the

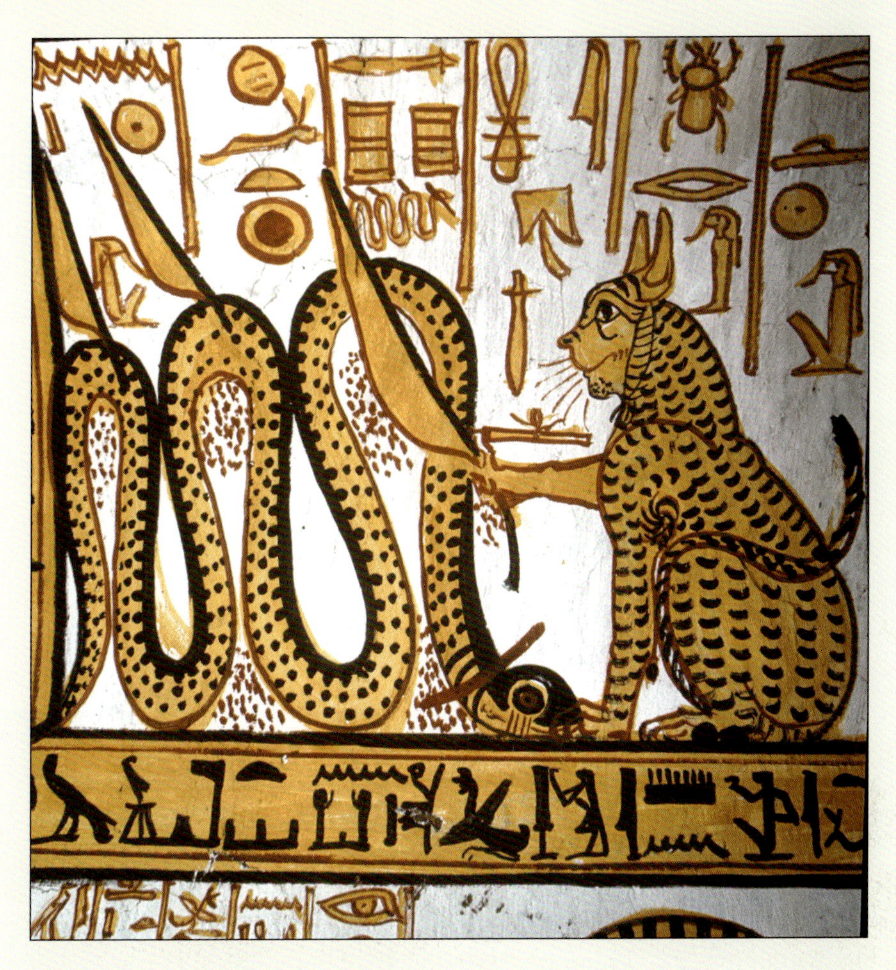

Taking the form of a cat, the ancient Egyptian sun god Ra slays Apophis, the serpentlike dragon that represents darkness and chaos. The painting, which dates to around 1200 B.C., comes from a tomb found near the ancient city of Thebes.

earthquakes and eruptions that seemed to defy explanation. They believed that when Typhon shifted under the rock, his movement caused the earth to quake; and when Mount Etna erupted, this was the dragon releasing his fiery breath.

Greek myths often feature a hero who battles the Western dragon. In one myth, the hero Perseus, who was the half-human son of Zeus, has a legendary fight with an evil dragon. The dragon had been ravaging the land, and the local villagers hoped to appease it by sacrificing a beautiful young woman named Andromeda to the dragon. When Perseus sees Andromeda chained to a rock by the sea, he immediately falls in love with her. Unable to let her die, Perseus agrees to slay the dragon in return for her hand in marriage. According to one retelling of the myth, soon there was an enormous roar from far out in the ocean, and a dragon appeared. It made its way to land, its gigantic jaw opened wide; steam and hot breath hissed from its mouth and nostrils. First Perseus threw stones at it, but to no avail. The dragon advanced and, as Andromeda looked on, helpless, it trapped Perseus between its enormous jaws and swallowed him whole. Within the beast's hideous belly, Perseus drew his adamantine sword—diamond edged—and cut his way out, killing it from the inside out."[15]

Norse Dragon Myths

From about A.D. 750 to 1050, Norse mythology developed in the northernmost part of Europe, which includes Sweden, Denmark, Norway, and Finland. In the Norse myths, dragons are enormous, aquatic monsters. Because of the dragon's link to the sea and its fierce nature, the Norse people used the dragon as a symbol of war. Warriors called Vikings sailed to raid European villages in longships called *drakkars* or dragon ships. Often these ships had a wooden dragonhead mounted on the ship's front as protection against sea serpents and other evil spirits.

The dragon is also closely linked to Norse creation and end-of-the-world myths. They believed that a giant ash tree linked and sheltered all the worlds and heavens. At the base of the tree, the dragon Nidhogg gnawed at the roots, hoping to break through and be released into the world. If Nidhogg succeeded, the Norse believed it would signal the end of the world.

Did You Know?

According to a popular legend from the Middle Ages, Saint Margaret of Antioch escaped from the belly of a dragon with the help of a cross. The cross so irritated the dragon's throat, the story goes, that the beast was forced to disgorge her.

One of the most famous Norse dragons is the Midgard Serpent, the child of the Norse trickster god Loki. The king of the Norse gods, Odin, cast the serpent into the sea because he feared its growing size

Dragon Gargoyles

Many medieval cathedrals in Europe have dragonlike gargoyles, carved in stone, on their outer walls and rooftops. Many wonder how something so closely associated with Satan and evil could come to rest on church walls.

According to legend, the link between church and dragon began in seventh-century northern France in the city of Rouen. In this tale a monstrous, slime-covered dragon emerges from the Seine River and enters the city. From its mouth, the dragon spews water to flood the town. The townspeople call it the *gargoule* or gargler. They flee the rushing water, but the archbishop stays firm and makes the sign of the cross in front of the dragon. Immediately, the dragon falls down, defeated. The archbishop leads the dragon back into town and burns it.

Since that day, European cathedrals remember the *gargoule* with carved stone gargoyles. They function as water spouts to drain water from parapet gutters and project it clear of the building's base. In this way, cathedral gargoyles share both a name and water-spouting ability from the *gargoule* dragon.

and power. Once there, the serpent grew so large it could wrap its body around the entire world and bite its own tail.

One day Odin's son Thor, the god of thunder, is fishing with the giant Hymir on the open sea. Thor had brought the head of Hymir's largest ox to use as bait. They row far out to sea, even though Hymir warns Thor that they might encounter danger from the Midgard Serpent. Thor hooks the ox's head on his line and casts it deep into the sea. The Midgard Serpent opens its jaws and swallows the bait whole. The serpent jerks its head so hard that even the mighty Thor is almost pulled overboard. As the serpent dives toward the sea bottom, Thor struggles with the line. The boat rocks, making huge waves in the ocean. At one point, Thor plants his foot so firmly on the bottom of the boat that it breaks through the boat, and he is standing on the bottom of the ocean.

Finally, Thor pulls the sea dragon from the ocean bottom. Glaring at him, the serpent blows venom at him. Finally, Thor takes his enchanted hammer, meaning to strike and kill the monster. Hymir, however, is afraid of the monster and quickly cuts the fishing line with his knife. The dragon wiggles off the hook, slides back into the sea, and escapes. The Norse myth says that the Midgard Serpent still lies at the bottom of the ocean, where it will remain until the end of the world.

Dragons in the Bible

In the Bible, Western dragons appear as powerful monsters that only God and his angels can defeat. The Old Testament tells that God made a sea dragon called Leviathan on the fifth day of creation. Leviathan is a massive reptilian monster that lives in the depths of the ocean. Armored scales cover his back, protecting him from all weapons. According to the book of Job, Leviathan breathes fire. "Out of his mouth go forth firebrands; sparks of fire leap forth. From his nostrils issues steam, as from a seething pot or bowl. His breath sets coals afire; a flame pours from his mouth." According to the Bible's book of Isaiah, only God can kill Leviathan as the world ends on judgment day. "On that day, the Lord will punish with his sword that is cruel, great, and strong, Leviathan the fleeing serpent, Leviathan the coiled serpent; and He will slay the dragon that is in the sea."

In the New Testament, the dragon often represents the devil. In the book of Revelation, a dragon appears in the sky. "It was a huge dragon, flaming red, with seven heads and ten horns." The angels battle the dragon until it is overpowered and loses its place in heaven. The book of Revelation says that "the huge dragon, the ancient serpent known as the devil or Satan, the seducer of the whole world, was driven out; he was hurled down to earth and his minions with him." As Christianity spread through the Middle East, belief in many legendary creatures dwindled. Dragons, however, survived and became more fearsome.

Saint George and the Dragon

One of the most well known Western dragon myths involves the Roman soldier known as Saint George of Cappadocia (now Turkey). Saint George lived during the late third century, during the Emperor Diocletian's rule of the Roman Empire. He was a devout Christian, even though the Roman emperor worshipped pagan gods. When Diocletian started to persecute Christians, Saint George protested. He showed strength and courage when he refused to renounce his Christian religion under torture and was eventually beheaded.

According to the legend, Saint George is riding near the town of Silene, Libya, during one of his many travels as a soldier. There, a huge, winged dragon with a long spiraled tail lives in a nearby lake. The dragon crawls into the town, killing and eating anyone it sees. The dragon also gives off poisonous fumes that choke anyone who gets too close to it.

To appease the dragon, the villagers offered it sheep until it crawled away. Then the village began to run out of sheep. The dragon resumed its deadly rampages until the king agreed to the daily sacrifice of a child to the dragon. Meanwhile he was hoping and praying for a miracle to save his kingdom.

Did You Know?

Celtic dragons are strongly associated with water and often take the form of huge, winged sea serpents. Unlike other Western dragons, Celtic dragons usually have no legs.

The Dragon Is Slain

One day the king's own daughter is chosen to be sacrificed to the dragon. The princess is bound to a wooden stake at the edge of the swamp. As she waits for death, the princess hears a loud sound and fears the monster has arrived. Instead of the dragon, however, a tall knight appears. He is dressed in armor with a white breastplate and carries a lance and shield, decorated with a scarlet cross. The knight, Saint George, leaps from his horse and rushes to the princess.

When the princess explains her predicament to him, George pledges to defeat the dragon. The princess begs him to save himself, but George refuses. The dragon is evil come to life, everything that

George had pledged to conquer. As they talk, the dragon emerges from the lake. George had never seen a beast so evil or disgusting. It is dripping with stinking slime, oozing decay, and reeking of death. George leaps on his horse, makes the sign of the cross, and lifts his lance. Galloping at full speed, he charges the dragon. George thrusts his lance with all his strength at the beast, piercing its throat and pinning it to the ground.

The dragon is mortally wounded but not dead. George asks the princess for her belt. They bind the dragon with it, and the beast becomes as gentle as a lamb. Together they ride back to the king's castle, leading the subdued dragon on a leash.

The king and his people rejoice to see the princess alive but are terrified to see the dragon again. George reassures them and promises that if they abandon the pagan Roman religion, convert to Christianity, and are baptized, he will slay the dragon. When the king and the villagers agree, George draws his sword and cuts off the dragon's head.

Did You Know?

According to legend, the archangel Saint Michael, considered the most powerful defender of God's people, slew many dragons. European churches dedicated to the saint were often built on mountaintops, which were believed to be the home of dragons.

All That Is Evil

Because the dragon was seen as the embodiment of Satan, European myths and folklore often tell of Christian knights fighting dragons to prove themselves and their bravery. According to Carol Fontaine, professor of biblical theology and history at the Andover Newton Theological School, "We often find in stories that the best heroes are the ones who have the most outrageous and formidable enemies to fight. So the dragon made a wonderful foil for Christian knights who had to prove themselves and prove the power of their religion over the old pagan religions."[16] The fearful image of a dragon also became an easy way for clergy to portray evil vividly and forcefully to churchgoers.

In medieval times, stories of dragons multiplied across the European continent. Before long, every hamlet and village in Europe had its own dragon story. These tales told of fierce dragons burning crops in the fields and terrorizing villages and maidens. Knights

According to legend, the Roman soldier and devout Christian known as Saint George saved a town from a vicious dragon. A painting from the 1500s depicts Saint George thrusting his lance into the dragon's throat and pinning it to the ground.

Dragon Slayers

While dragons instilled fear in the hearts of many, some dragon stories feature brave souls who search out these monsters to kill them. If successful, dragon slayers win fame, glory, and the potential for collecting a dragon's treasure. Along with Saint George and Beowulf, several heroes became legendary dragon slayers.

In one story, the Greek demigod Hercules faces the Hydra of Lerna, a creature with nine dragon heads. Every time Hercules cuts off one of the Hydra's heads, two more grow back in its place. Hercules eventually uses fire to singe the stumps before new heads can grow back. Then he cuts off the final head, slaying the Hydra.

In another legend from around A.D. 210, the Austrian giant Haymo is called on to protect the people of Innsbruck from a dragon that guards a large treasure hoard in a nearby mountain. Haymo dons his armor and attacks the dragon. The dragon retreats to its lair with Haymo following. Eventually Haymo slays the dragon and cuts off its tongue for proof, making him famous throughout the land.

searched for dragons to prove their courage and valor. Images of the dragon appeared in murals, tapestries, and stained glass windows. Drawings of dragons spread across the pages of handwritten illuminated manuscripts.

In many stories and images, the Western dragon terrorized the people with its fiery breath. At the same time, medieval art often pictured the mouth of hell as a great monster with flames spouting from inside. With the dragon representing evil and Satan, "it seems natural that there is an association between hell fire and dragon fire so far as Christian dragons are concerned,"[17] says Joe Nigg, a historian who researches mythical creatures.

Feared in many myths, the Western dragon is a great monstrous beast that battles gods and humans. Scaly and serpentine, it grows legs, wings, and a barbed tail. It breathes fire and soars across the sky. The dragon terrorizes villages, hoards treasure, and battles gods and knights to the death. It is little wonder that the Western dragon became a physical representation of all that was evil and feared in the world.

Chapter 3

Magical Dragons of the East

In contrast to the fear and loathing felt for the Western dragon, myths and legends from eastern lands such as China, Japan, and Korea characterize the dragon as a benevolent and kind beast. Instead of being despised by ancient peoples in these areas, dragons were valued for their magic, beauty, and intelligence. For more than 3,000 years, these wise creatures have held a place of honor in the cultures of East Asia.

In myths, Eastern dragons often represent the mighty power of nature. They breathe clouds and move the seasons. They are also thought to be intimately connected with water and can control rivers, lakes, seas, and rain.

While these powerful creatures usually demonstrate wisdom and kindness, they can have a darker side. Insult or lack of respect can lead a dragon to use its power over nature to cause horrific natural disasters such as drought, flood, and hurricanes.

Characteristics of the Eastern Dragon

In the stories of East Asia, the dragon is closely associated with life-giving water in the form of rain, lakes, rivers, and oceans. The idea of the dragon as a weather god or a protector of water surfaced in China sometime between 3500 B.C. and 2000 B.C. Many stories from that time depict dragons as living in splendid underwater palaces. In artists' depictions, these water-dwelling beasts often have elongated bodies reminiscent of water snakes. In other stories, Eastern dragons make their homes in the sky, especially in rain clouds.

In Eastern myths, dragons rarely scorch the earth or an enemy with fire-breath. Instead, they use the power of nature, such as a crushing flood, to punish those who oppose them. Dragon lore says that some of the worst floods and storms in history began when a human upset a dragon.

One of the most amazing characteristics of the Eastern dragon is its ability to shape-shift, or transform itself into another form. In Eastern myths, dragons often choose animal forms such as fish, snakes, dogs, rats, and cows. They also transform into human beings, usually becoming a wizened old man or a beautiful young woman. According to legend, a shape-shifting dragon can be detected in several ways. One method is to cook a suspected fish. If it shines a five-colored light or speaks in a human voice, it is sure to be a transformed dragon.

Another common characteristic of the Eastern dragon is its ability to fly without wings. Instead, a magic pearl hidden beneath its

Stories from Korea, China, and Japan portray dragons as benevolent creatures who are valued for their magic, beauty, and intelligence. A painting that hangs in a Buddhist temple in Korea depicts a meeting between a monk and a dragon.

chin gives the dragon the power to fly and rise to heaven. Sometimes called the Pearl of Knowledge, the pearl is also thought to contain the dragon's vast wisdom. Others say the Eastern dragon's ability to fly comes from its *chi'ih muh*, a bladderlike swelling or bump on top of its head.

Explaining Weather

Eastern myths commonly use dragons to explain weather phenomena. Centuries ago, people in China and Japan believed that a dragon must fly up to the sky to form a cloud that would bring rain to the land. In times of drought, the Chinese and Japanese tried to convince the dragon to leave its earthly pool and bring rain. Sometimes they beat gongs to summon the dragon. Other times they stirred dragon ponds with iron rods because they believed that dragons were afraid of iron and would fly skyward to escape the metal. Other times, people tried to encourage the dragon to fly and bring rain by frightening it with images of the Garuda, a mythical half eagle, half human creature and enemy of dragons.

Did You Know?

Long ago, if an ordinary citizen of China was caught displaying a dragon with five toes, he or she could be put to death because only the emperor's dragon could have five toes.

Other myths explain how dragons cause storms and floods. Dragons fighting in the water stir floods that ravage the land. Dragons fighting in the air trigger violent storms in the sky. During these storms, the heavens send lightning flashes to stop the dragon fight. In other legends, thunderstorms form when a baby dragon hatches from its egg and whirls in the sky on its ascent to heaven.

Eastern legends also explain the seasonal nature of storms by attributing them to the movement of dragons between the heavens and seas. In the spring, many dragons live in the heavens. In the fall, they return to live in their underwater palaces. The passing between sea and sky creates the destructive storms.

The Chinese Dragon

One of the most famous Eastern dragons is the Chinese dragon, with its serpentine body and bearded face. According to Chinese myth,

The Dragon Gate

In Japan, a widely known myth shows the traditional association of Eastern dragons and water. Each year, legend says, the golden koi, or carp, swim upstream for the length of the Yellow River until they reach a mountain waterfall called the Dragon Gate. There, the fish gather beneath the waterfall. They try to leap over the falling water and reach the calmer stream above. In their attempts, many fish fail. However, those that successfully leap above are said to transform into magnificent dragons and fly high into the sky. This legend is the basis for a common Japanese proverb for students. When they pass important tests in school, they are said to have "passed the Dragon Gate." The Dragon Gate has become a symbol of achieving success in a person's life or career.

four main types of dragons rule the earth and the sky. The *t'ien lung*, or celestial dragon, protects the heavens; the *shen-lung*, or spiritual dragon, rules the sky; the *ti-lung* dragon controls the land, streams and rivers; while the *fu-ts'ang lung*, or treasure dragon, hoards jewels and metals in the deepest caves under the earth's surface.

According to the Chinese scholar Wang Fu, who lived during the Han dynasty (206 B.C.–A.D. 220), each of these Chinese dragon types is a combination of nine beasts. Karl Shuker, a leading expert on the study of dragons, further explains: "The Chinese dragon's head is that of a camel, its eyes are a demon's, its ears a cow's, its horns are the branched antlers of a stag, its neck is a snake's, its belly a clam's. The soles of its feet are a tiger's, while its claws are an eagle's, and the 117 scales sheathing its long body are those of a carp."[18]

Experts believe that Chinese dragons may have developed from the people's ancient respect for the sky as the source of water, sunshine, storms, and wind. Essential rain watered rice fields that were the lifeblood and cornerstone of Chinese society. The dragon became the controller of these rains, bringing life to the fields. In addition, Chinese dragons also act as benevolent protectors in myths. They have the power to ward off evil spirits, protect the innocent, and grant safety to all people.

While it is primarily kind, the Eastern dragon can at times be malevolent and cruel. The dragon's immense power can destroy, causing great storms that batter the Chinese lands. In some legends, the dragon uses its power over water to bring about floods, droughts, and tidal waves.

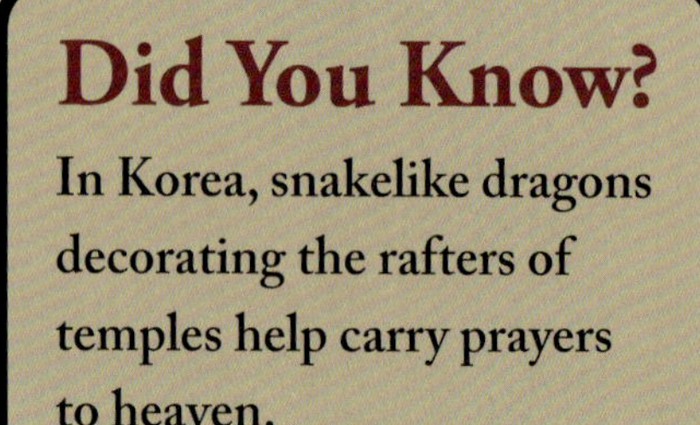

Did You Know?
In Korea, snakelike dragons decorating the rafters of temples help carry prayers to heaven.

Chinese legend explains that the dragon's changing nature comes from its 117 scales, which balance its good and evil traits. "Of these scales, 81 are infused with benevolent essence (yang) and 36 with malign essence (yin),"[19] Shuker explains. Because the majority of the dragon's scales are filled with good essence, it behaves most of the time in a kind and benevolent way. Sometimes, however, the malicious side of the dragon overpowers the good and causes it to use its power to harm and destroy.

The Legend of the Four Dragons

Several Chinese myths explain how China's land and waters were made. One of the most famous legends tells how dragons formed China's four great rivers. When the tale begins, China does not have any rivers, and the land is dry. The people rely on rain to water and grow their crops. One year, the rain stops falling, and a devastating drought overcomes the land. Crops shrivel and dry up. Without crops for food, the people begin to starve.

Four dragons that live in the eastern sea—the black dragon, the long dragon, the pearl dragon, and the yellow dragon—see the people's suffering and decide to help. They scoop water from the sea and spray it into the sky. This water falls as if it is rain. The thirsty crops drink the water and blossom once again.

But the dragons' action angers the god of the sea, for they had taken his water without asking his permission. The god of the sea tells China's emperor that the dragons stole from him. The emperor decides to punish the dragons and imprisons them under four mountains. And so the dragons, determined to keep supplying the people with desperately needed water, turn themselves into four rivers. The Chinese people use this story to explain how China's four great rivers—the Black River, the Long River, the Pearl River, and the Yellow River—were formed.

Gift of Knowledge

Myths portray Eastern dragons as wise and intelligent. At times, the dragons share knowledge with humans. In one of the earliest Eastern dragon legends, a dragon-horse with scales and wings emerges from the Lo River around the year 2962 B.C. Eight black spots in various designs decorate the dragon's back. The Chinese emperor Fu Hsi sees the dragon and its strange markings. When Fu Hsi arrives home, he draws the eight designs he saw on the dragon's back.

These designs became the eight primary characters, or trigrams, that formed the basis of the Chinese written language. The dragon was said to have shared the secret of writing and civilization with Fu Hsi. The emperor then shared the dragon's gift with the people of China, teaching them how to write. He also taught the people to cook, make music, fish with nets, and hunt with iron weapons. In some versions of the legend, Fu Hsi himself is part man, part dragon with the head of a man and the body of a serpent.

> **Did You Know?**
>
> **In Borneo in Southeast Asia, the dragon is a goddess of the underworld. She protects the living and guards the dead.**

In another legend, a dragon uses its wisdom to solve a problem for the people of China. Emperor Yu had not been able to stop terrible floods that devastated the country. Disguised as a great bear, he comes to a remote cliff to think. Looking over the waves, Yu sees a huge dragon flying his way. Yu recognizes the dragon as a water spirit who lives in the great storm clouds. He tells the dragon of his troubles with the flood. Offering to help, the dragon strikes a rock with its tail

The bearded dragon with a serpentine body is frequently seen in artwork from China. This image appears in a Chinese temple in Malaysia.

and breaks the rock into a hundred pieces. Together, the bear and dragon work, the dragon breaking rocks and the bear moving the pieces away. After three years of labor, the dragon splits the last rock. The floodwaters rush through the channel that Yu and the dragon have made in the cliff, leaving acres of flat, fertile soil. Yu thanks the dragon and takes human form once again.

Imperial Dragon

Honored above all other creatures for its wisdom and power, the Chinese dragon became a symbol of imperial rule. For more than 2,000 years, Chinese emperors were known as the True Dragon, Son of Heaven. Images of dragons decorated the royal palace, clothing, household goods, and ritual objects. The royal coat of arms showed two dragons fighting for a pearl. The emperors sat on a dragon throne and wrote with a pen called the dragon's brush. The emperors' hands were even called dragon's claws.

The people believed that a wise emperor united heaven and earth in harmony, bringing peace and prosperity to the land. The poet Qu Yuan wrote that one of the legendary Five Emperors, Huang-ti (2697–2598 B.C.), was flown to heaven by a team of dragons, solidifying the emperor's connection to dragons and the heavens.

Several Chinese myths explain the origin of the dragon and emperor connection. In one story, a poor farmer lives in rural, rugged land, far from the great cities of China. One day, as he comes home from the fields, he passes by a pond. There he sees his wife sleeping on the banks of the pond and a great dragon hovering above her. The sky darkens with clouds, lightning flashes, and thunder rumbles. Months later, the farmer's wife gives birth to a beautiful baby boy, whom they name Liu Pang. The farmer and his wife are filled with great joy; they believe their son to be a gift from the dragon.

Liu Pang eventually grows up to become the first ruler of the Han dynasty, Emperor Gaozu, who ruled from 202 B.C. to 195 B.C.

Counting Dragon Toes

Counting the toes on an Eastern dragon can give a clue as to where it originated. Chinese dragons typically have five toes. Three toes means the dragon comes from Japan. Korean dragons have four toes. Each culture has a legend to explain this difference. The Chinese say that dragons appeared first in China. As they spread to Korea and Japan, they lost toes. The Chinese dragon never reached the West because it lost all its toes before it could get there.

The Japanese and Koreans have a slightly different explanation. The Japanese say that the dragon first appeared in their country with three toes. As it moved to Korea and China, the dragon grew new toes. According to the Japanese, the Eastern dragon never reached the West because it would have grown too many toes to walk. Similarly, Korean legend says that the four-toed dragon originated in Korea and then lost a toe as it moved to Japan and grew a toe as it traveled into China.

Historians believe that Liu Pang may have claimed to descend from dragons in order to invent a noble lineage for himself. His invented dragon ancestor was more acceptable in traditional China than his true peasant background. According to Yunxiang Yan, professor of anthropology at UCLA, "When Liu Pang and his associates took power; they felt the need to justify, to legitimize this new dynasty and to upgrade Liu Pang's nobility. Therefore, they give this new component of dragon mythology. And from that day onward, the dragon becomes the symbol of imperial power."[20]

The Japanese Dragon

Like the dragons of Chinese lore, the dragons of Japanese mythology are large, wingless creatures with serpentlike bodies and clawed feet. The Japanese dragon is also associated with the emperor and is often used as the emperor's symbol. In fact, Emperor Hirohito, who ruled from 1926 until his death in 1989, traced his ancestry back 125 generations to Princess Fruitful Jewel, known as the daughter of a dragon king of the sea.

The Japanese dragon is primarily a sea god. This difference may have arisen because the islands of Japan are less vulnerable to drought than China. Therefore, the Japanese people had less need to pray to a dragon-god to bring rain.

In Japanese mythology, Dragon King Ryujin lives in an underwater sea palace near the Ryuku Islands. Built from red and white coral, the dragon king's palace is guarded by dragons and full of treasure. Among the dragon king's treasures are the Tide Jewels, which control the ebb and flow of the ocean's tides. In one legend, the Empress Jingu plans an invasion of Korea. She prays to Ryujin and asks him to give her the Tide Jewels. When the dragon king grants her wish, the empress sails with her fleet to Korea. When the Korean fleet sails to meet her ships, Empress Jingu casts the Low Tide Jewel into the ocean. The tide immediately recedes, leaving the Korean ships stuck in the sand and mud. As the Korean sailors jump out of their ships onto the sand, the empress throws the High Tide Jewel into the ocean. A tidal wave appears and drowns the Koreans. The wave carries the empress's Japanese ships to the Korean harbor and to victory.

In addition to being connected with the sea, Japanese dragon lore is closely associated with Buddhist temples found throughout Japan. In myths, many dragons live in bodies of water near temples. Many temple names include dragon references such as the Tenryu-ji, or Heavenly Dragon Temple. In addition, dragon sculptures decorate Buddhist temples. The dragon images represent obstacles that humans must overcome in life before they can attain enlightenment. Every October, dancers perform the Kinryu-no-Mai or Golden Dragon Dance

Did You Know?

Japanese samurai warriors wore body armor decorated with dragons. The dragon in Japan was a symbol of masculine power.

at the Sensoji Temple in Asakusa, Japan. According to temple legend, 1,000 pine trees suddenly appeared overnight near the temple. Three days later, a golden dragon descended into the pine trees from the heavens. Held to bring good fortune and prosperity, the annual dance celebrates the temple's founding in A.D. 628.

Dragons in Korea and Vietnam

Other Asian countries also have a rich tradition of dragons and dragon lore. Korea has three main types of dragons. The Yong is the most powerful and protects the sky. The Yo lives in the ocean, and the Kyo is found in the mountains. The Korean dragon has the eyes of a rabbit, the belly of a frog, 81 scales on its back, and four claws.

The dragons of Korea are said to have the eyes of a rabbit, the belly of frog, a back covered in scales, and four claws. The three most important dragons in Korean mythology live in the sky, the ocean, and the mountains.

In Vietnam the dragon is commonly called Con Rong or Con Long. Vietnamese artists frequently feature the dragon in paintings and sculptures. According to one Vietnamese legend, when the Vietnamese were fighting barbaric invaders from the north, the gods sent dragons to help protect and defend the land. The dragons spit jewels and jade into the sea, which formed a group of small islands and reefs that became a natural fortress against invaders. The bay became known as Ha Long or Descending Dragon. Today it is a popular tourist site in Vietnam.

Did You Know?

The ancient Chinese traded a substance said to be dragon saliva to use in making perfume.

Descendants of the Dragon

Many experts believe that the Eastern dragon evolved in myth and legend to explain natural phenomena like floods and droughts. How a culture viewed nature may explain how it characterized its dragons. In the East, the people sought to live in harmony with the forces of nature. As a result, the Eastern dragon emerged as a powerful human ally.

Although most people no longer believe in dragons as real creatures, many remnants of dragons can be found in Eastern cultures. In towns and cities, dragon images decorate temples, palaces, walls, and bridges. Modern festivals honor and celebrate the dragon with dragon boat races and dragon dances. In China, the people still call themselves Lung Tik Chuan Ren, or descendants of the dragon. In these ways, the Eastern dragon lives on.

Chapter 4

Animals That Inspired Dragon Myths

Stories about dragons have fascinated people throughout the ages. Dragon images can be found on the Ishtar Gate of Babylon, scrolls from China, and in Egyptian hieroglyphs. They adorn Ethiopian drawings, decorate Viking ships and Aztec temples, and tower on cliff paintings above the Mississippi River.

How could so many cultures that had no contact with each other create such similar beasts? Perhaps they uncovered dinosaur bones and created myths to explain the extraordinary skeletons. Maybe living animals such as lizards or crocodiles formed the basis of dragon myths. One of the most intriguing possibilities is that dragons were based on living creatures that have yet to be discovered by science.

"Dragon Bones"

Today, most people believe that dragons are imaginary beasts; though entertaining, dragon lore is viewed as pure fiction. At the heart of many legends, however, may be a grain of truth. Stories grow from that tiny seed, multiplying and expanding with each storyteller's imagination and retelling. Dragon legends probably grew out of the stories people told about sightings of strange and unfamiliar animals or unexplained events.

Long before the study of fossils became the science of paleontology, people found fossilized bones in Asia, Europe, and the Americas. Many believed that these bones were the remains of dragons from long ago. "Bones exposed by storms, earthquakes, or digging were well known to the ancients," says Adrienne Mayor, professor of folklore at Princeton University. "Some extinct mammals have startlingly dragon-like skulls, and Asian dragon myths may be based

Experts believe that real animals might have been mistaken for dragons in ancient times. The giant green iguana (pictured)—with its scaly body, a ridge of spines along its back, and a flap of skin below its neck—could easily have been seen as a dragon.

Dinosaur fossils such as this Tyrannosaurus rex *skull could have led ancient peoples to believe that they had uncovered dragon bones. Fossilized animal heads with massive jaws and teeth or horns along with other fossil finds would have strengthened the belief in dragons.*

on . . . fossils, which were at one time universally known as 'dragon bones,'"[21] adds Moyer. Some experts suggest that the skulls of cave bears, half as big as grizzlies, could have been the basis of dragon tales. Other "dragon bones" may have belonged to dinosaurs.

Dinosaurs and Dragons

In many ways, dinosaurs resemble the most common depictions of dragons. Dinosaurs like *Tyrannosaurus rex*, or *T. rex*, had enormous size and power. Many types of dinosaurs protected themselves with fierce, sharp teeth and tough armorlike skin. On the stegosaur, plates stood on its back like spikes. Large horns protruded from a triceratops's head like dragon horns.

The ferocious *T. rex* may be the dinosaur most similar to the dragon. *T. rex* was one of the largest carnivores to walk the earth. It grew up to 40 feet (12.2m) long and towered 15 to 20 feet (4.6m to 6.1m) in the air. Strong thighs and a powerful tail helped *T. rex* move quickly after its prey. Scientists believe that *T. rex* could eat up to 500 pounds (227kg) of meat in a single bite. It had serrated, conical teeth that could easily pierce and rip the flesh of its prey.

Although not technically a dinosaur, pterosaurs that lived during the dinosaur age were also dragonlike creatures. These winged reptiles ruled the skies. Some grew as large as an airplane and had a wingspan of about 40 feet (12.2m). These predators had long, narrow heads, large eyes, and small, sharp teeth. Their smaller bodies were built for flight with lightweight, hollow bones. Bony crests on their heads may have acted as a rudder when flying. They could flap their wings, which were covered by a leatherlike membrane. Meat-eating pterosaurs devoured fish, crabs, and some small land animals. Like a dragon, they swooped from the sky to grab their prey.

After they died out, dinosaurs and winged reptiles left their bones as a record of their presence. Fossils of dinosaurs and pterosaurs have been found on several continents. As early humans stumbled upon skeletons and fossils of these incredible creatures, they probably could not imagine what animal could have left the bones. With only a small leap of the imagination, early humans may have decided that they had found dragon bones.

Did You Know?

The skull of a woolly rhinoceros, once kept in the town hall of Klagenfurt, Austria, was said to be the remains of a dragon slain before the city's founding around 1250.

Reptilian Cousins

In addition to dinosaurs, reptiles that have existed for centuries share many characteristics with the mythological dragon. Crocodiles, alligators, and giant lizards with their scaly skin, large teeth, and long, powerful tails could have created fear in ancient peoples. In countless retellings of stories, these real creatures may have grown wings and learned how to breathe fire, becoming dragons. Asian dragons

Myth Becomes Reality: Discovery of the Komodo Dragon

In the early twentieth century, inhabitants of a few remote Indonesian islands told tales of a dragonlike beast. In their stories, the creature was sheathed in scales, had sharp talons, and stalked human prey. Westerners arriving on the island scoffed at the native tales. They thought such an animal could not possibly exist. Instead, they believed it had been born in the imagination of the island people and persisted through the years in local superstitions. One day in 1912, however, the Westerners learned how wrong they had been. A Dutch army officer came face to face with this real-life dragon that stretched 10 feet (3m) long. Zoologists named this species of monitor lizard a Komodo dragon. It is the biggest living lizard in the world today.

The Komodo dragon is an ancient reptile with clay-colored, scaly skin. It walks on short, bowed legs and swings a huge, muscular tail. The reptile also has a long, yellow, forked tongue that mimics a dragon spitting fire. The Komodo dragon eats wild pigs, deer, buffalo, snakes, fish, and other animals. To hunt, the dragon will hide along a trail and wait for unsuspecting prey to walk by. Then the dragon attacks with long claws and sharp teeth. The dragon's bite contains deadly bacteria that poison the victim. If the prey escapes, the Komodo dragon will follow until the poison takes effect, killing its prey.

in particular share a striking resemblance to the Chinese alligator. Both creatures are long and thin and spend much of their time in the water.

Some of the biggest and most vicious lizards alive today are the monitor lizards of Africa, Asia, and Australia. According to dragonologist and researcher Karl Shuker, these creatures "would have been particularly effective as models for such monsters [dragons]."[22] While some monitors are less than a foot long, the largest monitor lizard can grow up to 10 feet (3m) long and weigh over 350 pounds (159kg). Sometimes very hostile, monitor lizards will lash out with their strong tails at the slightest provocation. In addition, these lizards can severely injure with their long, sharp claws. Meat-eating monitor lizards will devour anything they can reach, dismembering their prey with their strong jaws.

In addition to looking like dragons, monitor lizards also display dragonlike behaviors. Many monitors hold their heads erect on long necks, which makes them seem alert and intelligent. They climb and swim with ease. When facing an enemy, a monitor lizard opens its mouth and inflates its neck to make it look larger than it really is. The lizard hisses to scare prey and rises on its hind legs before attacking. Like a dragon, it can deliver deadly blows with its tail.

Models from the Sea and Sky

The animal world is filled with creatures that could have been mistaken for dinosaurs by people who had no way of knowing otherwise. Whales, giant squid, and sharks could easily have been confused with dragons by sailors of long ago.

Did You Know?

Frilled dragons and bearded dragons, small lizards from Australia that resemble tiny dragons, are popular pets among lizard lovers.

The moray eel, which lives in tropical and temperate seas worldwide, has a long, muscular, snakelike body that averages about 5 feet (1.5m) long. The eels have wide, powerful jaws filled with long, sharp teeth that they use for killing and eating fish and mollusks. Moray eels frequently hide in shallow water near reefs and rocks. One species of moray eel, the dragon moray, has horns on its head that give it a dragonlike appearance.

Another water creature, the giant salamander, lurks in freshwater brooks and ponds in the United States, China, and Japan. It is the largest living amphibian today and can grow up to 6 feet (1.8m) long in China. Giant salamanders have long, flexible bodies with tough, thick skin. An encounter with one of these real-life monsters could easily have inspired a story about Asian water dragons.

Some birds also could have been mistaken for dragons. Birds of prey such as eagles, vultures, and falcons hunt from the air. They use their keen vision to locate and track prey on the ground. These birds have large, powerful talons and beaks that enable them to easily tear and pierce their prey's flesh. Soaring overhead, vultures and other birds with large wingspans may have looked like dragons in flight to the people of ancient cultures.

Did You Know?

The sea dragon is a rare type of fish that lives off the coast of Australia. Only about 14 inches (35.6cm) long, it looks like a tiny swimming dragon.

A Terrifying Mix of Carnivorous Predators

David E. Jones, a professor of anthropology at the University of Central Florida in Orlando and author of *An Instinct for Dragons* (2000), suggests another reason that so many cultures have dragonlike creatures in their myths. He believes the dragon may be a composite of the carnivorous predators—pythons, big cats, and raptors—that fed on early humans and a response to man's innate primal fears of these predators.

Jones was studying vervet monkeys when he developed his theory. As he scanned pictures of the monkey's predators, Jones had a vision of the predators combining into one beast. "Suddenly, in my mind's eye, the three predator images merged. The leopard body took on the outer look of the python, resulting in a large reptilian body with four clawed feet and a mouth full of sharp teeth. When the wings of the martial eagle attached to the shoulders of the blended leopard/python, I saw a dragon!"[23] he said.

Jones points to the chimpanzee as evidence supporting his theory of innate primal fears. When an infant chimp encounters a snake, it is terrified even though it has never before seen the serpent creature. Jones says that the chimp's primate brain is wired for sensitivity to predators, even ones the individual has never seen. He believes that humans also share an innate primal fear of dragons even if they have never seen one. From this fear, Jones believes, humans created dragon stories.

Reinforcing the Belief in Dragons

Whether dragons were inspired by dinosaurs, reptiles, or innate primal fears, many people believed the mythical creatures existed even though they had never seen one. For centuries, scholars did not ask

Cryptozoology: The Study of Unknown Animals

Scientists called cryptozoologists spend their lives hunting for unknown animals. They search for living creatures that might exist today or may have existed in the past but have not yet been discovered. These potential, unknown creatures are called cryptids.

Cryptozoologists study myths and legends for clues to the possible nature of a real animal. They travel the globe to investigate folklore and personal accounts of unknown animals. Cryptozoologists know that not all sightings will turn out to be real animals. Some reports will be simply a combination of good storytelling, exaggeration, and honest mistakes.

Cryptozoologist Richard Greenwell traveled to the African Congo in the 1980s to hunt for sauropod dinosaurs. He thought that if these dinosaurs, which resembled dragons, had survived undetected, they could have been the basis for many dragon myths. Greenwell's long journey eventually proved unsuccessful, and he did not find any evidence of the sauropods. Still, many areas of the world are hard to reach. In these places, animals unknown to science may exist.

if dragons were real. Instead they asked, "why don't we see them anymore?" Pliny the Elder, a Roman author and naturalist who lived during the first century A.D., wrote that dragons did exist but lived in faraway India. He reported that they were large enough to drop out of trees and strangle elephants. At the time, Pliny's descriptions were treated as fact. They remained as truths for centuries, repeated by European scholars and naturalists.

These accounts from respected scholars strengthened the common person's belief in dragons as living creatures. In addition to scholarly reports, Bible stories reinforced people's belief in dragons. Devoutly religious people believed dragons existed because the Bible said they did.

Eyewitness encounters, however, were some of the most compelling arguments for the existence of dragons. People traveled to far-off lands and returned with descriptions of terrible dragonlike beasts. One of the earliest dragon sightings was reported by Herodotus, a Greek scholar. In the fifth century B.C., Herodotus traveled the world. Returning from Egypt and Arabia, he claimed to have seen skeletons of winged snakelike creatures.

Did You Know?

The Alaskan Inuit have legends of the *kikituk,* a dragonlike, seagoing reptile that walks ashore hunting humans.

Centuries later, as Europeans traveled more widely, they returned with detailed descriptions of horrible creatures. Even Marco Polo, one of the most well known and credible explorers of the late thirteenth and early fourteenth centuries, reported an encounter with a dragon. According to researcher Peter Hogarth, Polo described enormous serpents that were "ten paces in length and as thick as a cask, with two squat forelegs near the head, claws like those of a lion, enormous heads, eyes bigger than loaves, and a mouth that could swallow a man in one gulp."[24]

Some historians believe that such eyewitness accounts may have been based on sightings of actual animals. European travelers to Asia and Africa encountered exotic animals such as elephants and large reptiles for the first time. They brought back oral descriptions of these unfamiliar creatures. Without photographs, their descriptions

changed with each telling until the creatures took on many strange and exaggerated features. Charles Marshall, professor of paleontology at UCLA, believes that dragon stories may have started with actual sightings of alligators and crocodiles. "One of the characteristics of dragons are these big scales. I would say that alligators and crocodiles easily fit that,"[25] says Marshall. With a little imagination, exaggerated or misunderstood retellings of alligator or crocodile sightings could have easily birthed a dragon.

Crocodiles, such as the one pictured here, must have been a horrifying sight to ancient people who had little knowledge of the natural world. Exaggerated stories of encounters with creatures like this could have fueled tales of vicious dragons.

Could Dragons Exist?

Some people wonder if dragons could exist today but have remained hidden from scientists. For this to happen, the dragon would have to live in a well-hidden, remote place. Although much of the globe has been explored in recent history, a few places have still not been fully searched. Dragons living near the ocean floor, in deep underground caves, at the earth's poles, or high in the tallest mountain ranges could have remained hidden from human eyes.

Although this scenario is unlikely, some believe it is possible. Creatures dismissed as imaginary or extinct have been discovered alive before. In one case, the ancient Egyptians spoke of an okapi, or short-necked giraffe. The Western world had never seen the animal and dismissed it as a myth. Then in 1901 the myth became truth when European explorers found the animal alive in the African Congo.

The coelacanth fish also surprised scientists when they found it alive in the twentieth century. Scientists had believed that this ancient fish had gone extinct when the dinosaurs died out 65 million years ago. They were shocked when a coelacanth was found off Africa's coast in 1938. In recent decades, several other coelacanths have been caught. As recently as 2007 an Indonesian fisherman caught a coelacanth off the shores of Sulawesi Island.

If animals like the okapi and coelacanth can elude human detection for so many years, some wonder if a dragon might possibly do the same. The idea of dragons or dragonlike dinosaurs surviving in the hidden corners of the earth continues to spark the imagination of many.

Whether they exist or not, dragons remain a central part of the human experience through myth, art, and folklore. The dragon remains a symbol of human fear and the desire to understand and conquer those fears.

Chapter 5

Dragons in Pop Culture

For centuries, stories about dragons have been popular in myths, legends, and folklore. From the classic Greek myths to the English *Beowulf* poem, storytellers have written timeless tales about dragons and their interactions with humans.

Today, the dragon remains a fascinating figure for authors and filmmakers. New stories about dragons line the fantasy section of bookstores. Filmmakers are discovering new ways to bring the dragon to life in terrifying detail on the big screen. Whether portrayed as friend or foe, the dragon has made a lasting impression on popular culture.

A Fearsome Foe

Like storytellers from past generations, today's authors love to create stories about gigantic monsters that need to be confronted and killed. Terrible, powerful dragons that represent evil are a perfect choice, particularly in fantasy literature. Facing a dragon can provide page-turning conflict, danger, and adventure for the book's characters.

Smaug, the fire-breathing beast from J.R.R. Tolkien's *The Hobbit* (1937) may be one of the most frightening dragon villains to swoop from a book's pages. This enormously evil monster flies through the sky, tells riddles, and controls people with its seductive voice and hypnotic eyes. Smaug also guards an immense treasure in a cave hidden deep within a mountain.

In an illustration from one edition of The Hobbit, *Bilbo Baggins encounters Smaug, the fire-breathing dragon. J.R.R. Tolkien's 1937 book depicts the dragon as enormously evil and able to control people with its seductive voice and hypnotic eyes.*

In the book, a hobbit named Bilbo Baggins leaves his comfortable home on a quest to win a share of Smaug's treasure. On his journey, Bilbo meets a variety of creatures and characters. When Bilbo reaches the dragon's lair, he steals a gold cup from Smaug's treasure. This enrages the dragon. "Smaug came hurtling from the North, licking the mountain-sides with flame, beating his great wings with a noise like a roaring wind. His hot breath shriveled the grass before the door . . . [as] the dragon swooped and turned to pursue them."[26] Eventually, another character, Bard the archer, defeats Smaug by shooting an arrow through the one spot in the dragon's belly not protected by armorlike scales or a crust of jewels.

The timeless story earned Tolkien widespread critical acclaim. In 1938 the *New York Herald* awarded him a prize for best juvenile fiction. *The Hobbit* was also nominated that year for the Carnegie Medal in Literature, awarded annually to an outstanding book for children and young adults. In light of the book's success, Tolkien wrote sequels to the land of hobbits and dragons. Together, the three books became the Lord of the Rings trilogy.

More Dangerous Dragons

Dangerous dragons also appear throughout the Harry Potter series of books by author J.K. Rowling. Several different breeds of dragons inhabit Rowling's wizard world; they include varieties such as Common Welsh Greens, Norwegian Ridgebacks, Hungarian Horntails, and Chinese Fireballs. Each of these flying dragons is an enormous, fire-breathing beast with immense jaws and sharp talons. While the dragons in the Harry Potter series are not malevolent like Smaug, they are still dangerous and ferocious beasts. In addition, Rowling often uses dragon characters as guardians of treasure, like traditional Western dragons.

Did You Know?

The first name of wizard Draco Malfoy, one of Harry Potter's school rivals, means "dragon" in the Latin language.

In the first book, *Harry Potter and the Sorcerer's Stone*, Rowling introduces dragons when Hagrid the groundskeeper at Harry's school hatches a baby Norwegian Ridgeback dragon. The dragon's ferocious nature emerges when the newly hatched baby bites several characters, including its keeper, Hagrid, and Harry's best friend, Ron Weasley. Eventually, the baby dragon, named Norbert, is sent away to live in Romania where it will be under the care of specially trained wizards called dragon keepers.

Rowling's dragons appear again in terrifying detail in the fourth novel, *Harry Potter and the Goblet of Fire*. Harry has been chosen as one of the competitors in the Triwizard Tournament. In the tournament's first task, each of the competitors must steal an egg from a fierce and protective female dragon. Harry faces the fiercest dragon of the four, a Hungarian Horntail. As Harry approaches the fire-breathing dragon, he sees "her wings half-furled, her evil, yellow eyes upon him, a monstrous, scaly, black lizard, thrashing her spiked tail, leaving yard-long gouge marks in the hard ground."[27] Eventually, Harry uses his broom-flying skills to confuse the dragon and snatch her egg, but not before the deadly dragon slashes his shoulder with the spikes on her tail. In the seventh book of the series, *Harry Potter and the Deathly Hallows*, Harry and his friends again face a fierce dragon, this time guarding evil wizard Bellatrix Lestrange's vault at the wizard bank Gringott's.

Rowling's dragons exude danger, power, and terror just like the many dragons of old. In each encounter, her dragons test Harry Potter's courage and skill. By emerging victorious against the dragons, Harry can be compared with legendary dragon slayers such as Jason and Sigurd, who faced fierce dragons and won their treasures.

Did You Know?

Christopher Paolini wrote the first draft of his fantasy dragon adventure *Eragon* when he was only 15 years old.

An Unusual Friendship

Although authors like Tolkien and Rowling have created dragon opponents for their books' characters, other authors have explored a different relationship between dragons and humans. These dragons retain their fearsome characteristics but form a special bond with certain humans, helping them in times of trouble.

The Chinese Dragon Dance

One of the most well-known dragon images is the large parade dragon carried through the streets to celebrate the Chinese New Year. For centuries the Chinese people believed that the dragon controlled the rains. In China, where so many people depended on agriculture for their livelihood, rain was a necessity. Legend says that the people performed the first dragon dance to ask the Dragon King to release rain over their parched farmland. Today, the dance symbolizes the bringing of good luck and success in the New Year.

During the Chinese New Year celebration, teams of men and boy dancers carry brightly colored dragon forms on poles in a large parade down city streets. The dancers perform intricate dragon dances. One dancer moves the dragon's head while the others move its body. They lift, dip, thrust and sweep the dragon's head and mimic the movement of a dragon. Sometimes the dragon's head has animated features, controlled by one of the dancers. Music from drums, cymbals, and gongs accompany the dancing dragon's movements. Chinese tradition states that the longer the dragon, the more luck it will bring. As a result, some of the parade dragons are 100 feet (30.5m) long.

Author Anne McCaffrey has created an entire world of dragons that bond with humans in her Dragonriders of Pern books written between 1968 and 2002. The fire-breathing dragons of Pern look like enormous reptiles with wings, but they also have a special relationship with some humans. These dragons are smart and can telepathically bond with their riders. Together the dragons and riders fight the Thread, an enemy that threatens Pern. The bond between dragon and rider is so strong that if the rider dies, the dragon will commit suicide.

A fierce Hungarian Horntail dragon chases Harry Potter during the Triwizard Tournament, in this scene from the 2005 movie Harry Potter and the Goblet of Fire. *The movie is based on the book of the same name by J.K. Rowling.*

The relationship between a human and a dragon is also featured in Christopher Paolini's best-selling Inheritance Cycle trilogy of books, *Eragon* (2003), *Eldest* (2005), and *Brisingr* (2008). In the first book, a 17-year-old farm boy named Eragon discovers a mysterious blue object. It turns out to be a dragon egg that hatches to become Saphira, a blue-scaled dragon. According to a prophecy, Eragon's destiny is to become a dragon rider like the ancient protectors of the kingdom. Eragon's connection to the dragon becomes apparent early in the story, as Paolini describes: "Saphira was a balm for Eragon's frustration. He could talk freely with her; his emotions were completely open to her mind, and she understood him better than anyone else."[28] Together, Eragon and Saphira travel on a series of adventures, seeking to join others in the fight to overthrow the evil king and restore peace to the land.

Best-selling author Cornelia Funke has also created a dragon-human friendship in her book *Dragon Rider* (2004). Her novel tells the story of Firedrake, a young dragon that sets out on a dangerous journey to the mythical Rim of Heaven, a place where silver dragons can live peacefully, away from the threat of destruction by mankind. On the journey, Firedrake is joined by his fairylike brownie friend Sorrell and a lonely human orphan named Ben. When Ben volunteers to help Firedrake, he has no idea that he is at the center of an ancient dragon prophecy about a Dragon Rider who will save the dragons. The unlikely group bonds and works together to face many dangers and the ever-present threat of an evil dragon hunter that is tracking them, intent on destruction.

From Books to the Big Screen

Leaping from the pages of books, dragons are now soaring into movies. Some films are based on books, while others are adventures created specifically for the big screen. Since the 1970s, dragons in many forms have thrilled and terrified moviegoers.

The dragon's transition from a book to the big screen, however, is a bit tricky. In books, authors create vivid images of enormous, and sometimes terrifying, dragons. A reader can imagine the dragon's flight, its scaly skin, and the heat from its fiery breath. On film, however, bringing a dragon to life is a challenge without a real-life model to copy. To solve this problem, some filmmakers choose to create the dragon as a cartoon character such as the dragons in the films *Shrek* (2001) and *Mulan* (1998).

Other filmmakers create lifelike dragons by using computer-generated images. Recent improvements in technology have allowed moviemakers to bring dragons to life in terrifying detail. These computer-generated images make dragons on film seem almost as realistic as human actors.

The fantasy adventure movie *Dragonheart* (1996) made an impression on moviegoers with its lifelike dragon sequences. It stars Dennis Quaid as dragon slayer Bowen and Sean Connery as the voice of the dragon Draco. The movie received mixed reviews but was generally praised for its visual effects. The dragon's realistically

Did You Know?

Dragon shrines and altars can still be seen in many parts of China and Japan, usually near seashores and riverbanks because most Eastern dragons were said to live in water.

Born in the Year of the Dragon

The Chinese zodiac is a rotating cycle of 12 years, with an animal representing each year. Traditionally, the 12 animals are, in order: rat, ox, tiger, rabbit, dragon, snake, horse, ram, monkey, rooster, dog, and pig. According to legend, the order of the animals was determined by a race held across a river. Each animal's position in the zodiac corresponds to the order it finished in the race.

Followers of the Chinese zodiac believe that the animal ruling the year of a person's birth will exercise a great influence on the person's life. The 12 animal signs are believed to represent different personality types. Each bestows its characteristics to those born under its sign. People born in 1988 and 2000 fall in the year of the dragon. The dragon is popular, respected, and a natural leader. It inspires trust and confidence and is good at giving orders. People born in the year of the dragon are thought to be energetic, intelligent, gifted, healthy, charismatic, noble, and brave. They can also display some of the dragon's negative characteristics, sometimes acting tactlessly or brashly.

fluid movements make viewers forget they are watching a computer-generated graphic instead of a living, breathing animal. Its close-up shots reveal frighteningly realistic teeth, perfectly synched speech, and subtle facial expressions. According to a *New York Times* reviewer, "The story's central fire-breathing creature is so well realized . . . that the human cast faces an uphill battle."[29] The movie's spectacular special effects earned it an Academy Award nomination for Best Visual Effects.

The dragon Saphira also steals the show in *Eragon* (2006), the movie adaptation of Christopher Paolini's book, starring Edward Speleers as Eragon and Rachel Weisz as the voice of Saphira. The dragon comes to life covered in muted blue scales, two horns, and a powerful, spiked tail. With two enormous feathered wings, filmmakers modeled Saphira's flight scenes after an eagle's flying patterns. One *USA Today* reviewer praised the computer-generated dragon, saying, "The most noteworthy character in *Eragon* is Saphira. The creature . . . is the undisputed star of a film that is predictable in its plot, clichéd in its dialogue, but stunning in its cinematography and production design."[30] The stunning dragon could not turn the movie into a box office success, however. *Eragon* grossed $249 million worldwide but fell short of studio expectations.

Terrifying on Television

The technology that allows dragons to come alive in movies has also trickled down to television. On the small screen, computer-generated dragons can speak, fly, and terrify in a new episode each week.

The popular SyFy Channel series *Merlin* features a prophetic and lifelike Great Dragon. In the show, the young magician Merlin arrives in the city of Camelot, which is ruled by the king, Uther Pendragon. The king has outlawed magic and holds the last dragon, the Great Dragon, prisoner deep under the city. Merlin meets the dragon, which tells him that Merlin's destiny is to protect Uther's son Arthur. In several episodes, Merlin consults the wise Great Dragon for advice and guidance. The show's third season was slated to begin in 2011.

Did You Know?

The Chinese dragon is one of the most popular tattoo designs used around the world.

Fascinating the Youngest Fans

With all the interest in dragons, middle school and elementary students want to read and learn about these mythical animals too. Books that are organized like dragon manuals have become very popular with these readers. These books do not narrate a story; instead, they claim to be the actual writings of a fictional dragonologist. Often presented in an encyclopedic format, they deliver the tiniest details about dragons to delight younger readers.

In a scene from the 2006 movie Eragon, *the young dragon rider known as Eragon spends a few quiet moments with Saphira, the dragon to which he is bound. The imaginary world of Eragon and Saphira was created by author Christopher Paolini.*

This is the case in *Dragonology: The Complete Book of Dragons* (2003), edited by Dugald Steer. This book claims to be the actual writings of English dragonologist Ernest Drake. Presented as a textbook for those who wish to study dragons, it treats dragons as if they were real objects of scientific study. It discusses the different species of dragon, diagrams the dragon's skeletal and muscular structure, and details the behavior and feeding habits of dragons. For the budding dragonologist, the book also covers how to work with dragons from tracking and finding one to taming and flying it. The matter-of-fact presentation of dragon material tones down the scare factor of these terrifying creatures, making it a good fit for younger readers.

The factual presentation in Lisa Trumbauer's *A Practical Guide to Dragons* (2006) makes learning about dragons interesting for younger readers. Sindri Suncatcher, a wizard apprentice, narrates the book through scrolls that detail what he has learned about dragons. Sindri's scrolls cover topics including dragon anatomy, combat techniques, society, and dragon language. Although loaded with facts, the narrator Sindri also slips a few moments of sly humor into the book, lightening the topic for the youngest readers. As one reviewer puts it, the resulting book "will provide hours of absorbed entertainment for humans in search of the nittiest grittiest details about dragons."[31]

For younger moviegoers, filmmakers make dragons less threatening by drawing them as cartoon characters. DreamWorks Animation's *How to Train Your Dragon* (2010) is loosely based on Cressida Crowell's book of the same name. In the movie, dragons fly over a mythical Viking village to plunder livestock and set houses on fire. The Vikings battle the dragons, and young boys can prove their bravery by killing one. The story twists when Hiccup, a scrawny Viking kid, downs a flying dragon during a battle. His compassionate nature leads him to set the dragon free rather than kill it. This gesture creates a bond between boy and dragon. Eventually, Hiccup and the dragon, named Toothless, join together to save Toothless's dragon clan and Hiccup's village from a menacing evil dragon. After their battle together, the war between the dragons and Vikings finally ends.

The film received positive reviews from critics and moviegoers. According to one reviewer, the movie was "a coming-of-age tale with surprising depth and a sweetly poignant tale of friendship between man and animal."[32] Within four months of its release the movie had earned more than $479 million worldwide.

Did You Know?

Author Anne McCaffrey created more than 100 differently named dragons in her Dragonriders of Pern series.

Timeless Popularity

From ancient myths to modern films, the human fascination with dragons shows no signs of diminishing. Today, authors create best-selling novels of dragon adventures. Modern technology makes the dragon appear more lifelike than ever in movies and television shows. Dragons can be found around the world from toys and clothing to expensive pieces of art.

On virtually every continent, dragons are an irresistible symbol of uncontrollable power and strength. As a powerful ally or the ultimate enemy, dragons have thrived in the imaginations of people around the world. These mythical and mysterious creatures are likely to entertain generations for years to come.

Source Notes

Introduction: The Mystery of Dragons

1. Quoted in John H. Lienhard, *Engines of Our Ingenuity*, "Topsell's Beasts," KUHF-FM Houston. www.uh.edu/engines/epi1586.htm.
2. Edward Topsell, *The History of Four-Footed Beasts and Serpents and Insects*, 1658; repr., New York: De Capo, 1967, p. 705.
3. Topsell, *The History of Four-Footed Beasts and Serpents and Insects*, p. 708.
4. Quoted in Karl Shuker, *Dragons: A Natural History*. New York: Simon & Schuster, 1995, p. 8.
5. Peter Hogarth, *Dragons*. New York: Viking, 1979, p. 5.

Chapter One: The Legendary Beast

6. Quoted in Hogarth, *Dragons*, p. 99.
7. Jonathan Evans, *Dragons*. New York: Metro Books, 2008, p. 166.
8. Topsell, *The History of Four-Footed Beasts and Serpents and Insects*, p. 706.
9. Quoted in AltonWeb, "Piasa Bird." www.altonweb.com.
10. Shuker, *Dragons: A Natural History*, p. 40.
11. Quoted in Johan Gunnar Andersson, *Children of the Yellow Earth: Studies in Prehistoric China*. New York: Taylor & Francis, 1973, p. 75.

Chapter Two: Deadly Dragons of the West

12. Shuker, *Dragons: A Natural History*, p. 54.
13. Shuker, *Dragons: A Natural History*, p. 55.
14. Hogarth, *Dragons*, p. 69.
15. Evans, *Dragons*, p. 112.
16. Quoted in, *In Search of History: Dragons*, DVD, The History Channel, 2002.
17. Quoted in, *In Search of History: Dragons*, DVD, The History Channel, 2002.

Chapter Three: Magical Dragons of the East

18. Shuker, *Dragons: A Natural History*, p. 86.

19. Shuker, *Dragons: A Natural History*, p. 86.
20. Quoted in *In Search of History: Dragons*, DVD, The History Channel, 2002.

Chapter Four: Animals That Inspired Dragon Myths

21. Quoted in Donald G. McNeil Jr., "From Many Imaginations, One Fearsome Creature," *New York Times*, April 29, 2003. www.nytimes.com.
22. Shuker, *Dragons: A Natural History,* p. 76.
23. David E. Jones, *An Instinct for Dragons*. New York: Routledge, 2000, p. 4.
24. Hogarth, *Dragons*, p. 113.
25. Quoted in *In Search of History: Dragons*, DVD, The History Channel, 2002.

Chapter Five: Dragons in Pop Culture

26. J.R.R. Tolkien, *The Hobbit*, e-book. London: HarperCollins, 1995, pp. 409–10.
27. J.K. Rowling, *Harry Potter and the Goblet of Fire*. New York: Scholastic, 2000, p. 353.
28. Christopher Paolini, *Eragon*. New York: Alfred A. Knopf, 2003, p. 60.
29. Janet Maslin, "Movie Review: *Dragonheart* (1996)," *New York Times*, May 31, 1996. http://movies.nytimes.com.
30. Claudia Puig, "Cinematic Quest Falls a Little Short," *USA Today*, December 15, 2006. www.usatoday.com.
31. Emilie Coulter, "Amazon.com Review," Amazon. www.amazon.com.
32. Claudia Puig, "'Dragon': How to Do Smart Dialogue, 3-D Visuals the Right Way," *USA Today,* March 26, 2010. www.usatoday.com.

For Further Exploration

Books

Ernest Drake, *Drake's Comprehensive Compendium of Dragonology*. Boston, MA: Candlewick, 2009.

Joe Nigg, *How to Raise and Keep a Dragon*. Hauppauge, NY: Barron's, 2008.

David Passes, *Dragons: Truth, Myth and Legend*. London: Anova, 2007.

Catherine M. Petrini, *Dragons*. Farmington Hills, MI: KidHaven, 2007.

Sandra Staple, *Drawing Dragons: Learn How to Create Fantastic Fire-Breathing Dragons*. Berkeley, CA: Ulysses, 2008.

Lisa Trumbauer, *A Practical Guide to Dragon Riding*. Renton, WA: Mirrorstone, 2008.

Lisa Trumbauer, *A Practical Guide to Dragons*. Renton, WA: Mirrorstone, 2006.

DVD

In Search of History: Dragons, History Channel, 2006. This DVD takes viewers on a journey into the myths and legends of dragons. It includes the latest research on dragon myths and sightings, expert interviews, and dragon art from around the world.

Web Sites

Animal Planet: Dragons (http://animal.discovery.com/convergence/dragons). This Web site gives behind-the-scenes information and video clips from the making of the Animal Planet special *Dragons*. It also has sections about mythology, the science behind the dragon fantasy, and types of dragons.

Draconika (www.draconika.com). This Web site offers numerous articles about dragon history, mythology, famous dragons, physiology, and species of dragons.

The Dragon Chronicles (www.pbs.org/wnet/nature/episodes/the-dragon-chronicles/introduction/4517). The PBS show *Nature* examines the real-life origins of dragons. The Web site includes video clips, expert interviews, and information about animals that may have inspired the dragon.

The Dragon Stone (www.polenth.com). This Web site has a large collection of information about dragons, from dragon mythology to fantasy fiction. It offers dragon essays, retellings of myths and fairytales, and other dragon-related topics.

Here Be Dragons! (www.draconian.com/home/frameset.htm). This Web site has sections dedicated to types of dragons, dragon history, physiology, behavior, and mythology.

Index

Note: Page numbers in boldface indicate illustrations.

Picture Credits

Cover: iStockphoto.com
Ancient Art and Architecture Collection Ltd./ The Bridgeman Art Library International: 27
The Bridgeman Art Library International: 14, 60
iStockphoto.com: 17, 32, 37, 42, 46, 49, 50, 57
© Look and Learn/The Bridgeman Art Library International: 11, 21
Photofest/20th Century Fox: 68
Photofest/Warner Bros: 64
University of Houston Libraries, Courtesy of Special Collections: 7

About the Author

Carla Mooney is the author of many books for young adults and children. She lives in Pittsburgh, Pennsylvania, with her husband and three children.